VERY STRANGE PEOPLE

VERY STRANGE PEOPLE

James Cornell

SCHOLASTIC BOOK SERVICES
New York Toronto London Auckland Sydney Tokyo

ISBN 0-590-31331-2

Copyright © 1980 by James C. Cornell. All rights reserved. Published by Scholastic Book Services, a Division of Scholastic Magazines, Inc.

12 11 10 9 8 7 6 5 4 3 2 1   10   0 1 2 3 4 5/8
Printed in the U.S.A.   0 1

Contents

Very Strange People

Have you ever heard of the man who thought he was a teacup? Or the woman who built a house with hundreds of empty rooms and scores of staircases going nowhere? Or the aviator who fell out of his plane — and then right back into it again? Or the English noble who fed his dogs better than most people feed their friends? Or the cruel knight who made a bloody pact with the Devil?

These are only a few of the weird, unusual, sometimes funny and sometimes tragic people found in this book.

All of us have special traits, habits, or quirks of behavior that makes us different from our friends and relatives. For some, however, these odd quirks become so strong that the people become oddballs, laughed at by everyone, like Beckford the Mad Tower Builder of Britain.

Others become so obsessed with a goal or a dream that it takes over their lives, like Joshua Slocum, the first man to sail around the world alone. Still others, just by chance and for the wrong reasons, become legends, like Captain Kidd.

Sadly, some people let their eccentric ways turn to evil deeds, like Hetty Green, the Witch of Wall Street, or the infamous Giles de Ray. Fortunately, more people use their special talents to accomplish extraordinary feats, like Blondin the Daredevil of Niagara Falls or "Jerusalem" Whalley. And many use their unusual gifts to help their fellow men, like Vidocq, the criminal who became a master policeman, and Belzoni, the circus strongman who became an Egyptian explorer.

All the people you'll meet in this book — crackpots and criminals, clowns and crusaders, knights and knaves, bad guys and beautiful women — all had some special characteristic, something that set them apart from the crowd. Their schemes, their dreams, their crazy plans, wild plots, and silly escapades may thrill you or chill you, make you laugh or make you wonder. But no matter how you feel about them, you'll have to agree that all these characters are "very strange people"!

A Dog's Life

A dog's life wouldn't be a bad one if the pooch happened to be the pet of the Earl of Bridgewater.

The Earl, otherwise known as the Reverend Francis Henry Egerton, lived in Paris in the 1820s and exercised his wealthy eccentricity by entertaining his household of canine guests in a style fitting royalty.

Each night, his long banquet table was set for twelve dinner guests. At each place, dressed in appropriate finery and with a silk napkin tied about its neck, sat a favorite dog. Behind each pup stood a servant ready to attend to any special wants.

The dogs, perhaps realizing their honored position, behaved themselves perfectly, eating carefully from the plates like proper ladies and gentlemen. If, however, one of the dogs happened to forget its place and stole food from another's plate, or snarled at the lord, or bit one of the waiters, the misbehaving mutt was punished accordingly. The next day, the impolite pet was banished to another room, where, still dressed and served, it dined alone until it was sorry for its misdeeds and could return to the master's table.

After dinner, Lord Bridgewater liked to take his dogs for a ride through the streets of Paris. So, nightly, master and hounds, again all dressed properly, climbed into a carriage for a short jaunt. Just in case they might get out of the carriage into the dirty streets, Lord Bridgewater made certain that he and his canine passengers all wore leather boots. Moreover, he — and his dogs — put on brand-new boots *each day*, and those that had been worn once were carefully removed and arranged in order so he could count the days of the year by the line-up of boots in his hall.

The Pussycat Pirate

"**S**hip to the northeast! Closin' fast and flying the Jolly Roger! All hands on deck!"

The sailor high above in the crow's nest of the merchant ship bellowed out the bad news that danger had appeared on the horizon. A pirate galley, flying the dreaded skull-and-crossbones flag of the plunderer, was dead ahead and sailing on a direct course toward a confrontation at sea.

The merchant crew hastily gathered up whatever weapons they could muster and manned the few old, rusty cannons carried on board. They waited anxiously for the inevitable clash, ready to lose their precious cargo of spices and silks.

Miraculously, the expected raid never occurred. The pirate ship made some miscalculation and sailed right past the freighter, far off beyond cannon range. Its cannonballs and grapeshot fell ridiculously short of the target, splashing up some sea spray against the hull of the merchant ship, but doing no damage. By the time the pirates could change course and try for another attack, the merchant ship's sails had caught the wind and easily outdistanced the sea thieves.

Captain Kidd had flubbed again! Another prey had escaped because of his bungling, bad timing, and poor seamanship.

What? Captain Kidd a bumbler? Wasn't he the most successful pirate that ever lived? Wasn't he the terror of the seven seas, robbing ships at will, outwitting the navies of a dozen countries, and cruely making his victims walk the plank to watery graves?

Alas, most legends about Captain Kidd simply aren't true. The real-life William Kidd was really a pussycat, a man who didn't plan to be a pirate and, in fact, was not very good at it.

His fame and his fantastic image as a horrible scourge of the seas were the result of a political scandal, a sort of seventeenth-century Watergate, in which Kidd was the scapegoat, taking the blame for a plan of his employers.

In the late seventeenth century, when the great nations of Europe were dividing up the world into colonies, thousands of ships laden with gold, jewels, spices, fine fabrics, and other treasures sailed between remote lands and the busy ports of England, France, Spain, and Portugal.

Unfortunately, all these nations competed for the same prizes, often to the point of war. When wars broke out, the rulers of these far-flung empires could not always provide enough battleships and destroyers to protect their freighters on the open seas.

In places like the West Indies and the Indian Ocean — where the cargoes were very rich and the naval support very meager — pirates flourished, preying on unprotected merchant ships. Ports such as Port Royale in Jamaica and St. Marie Island just north of Madagascar, in the Indian Ocean, became notorious pirate strongholds.

Although the pirates operated all over the world, most of their supplies came from New York and Boston. Indeed, many American ship chandlers, including a New Yorker named Robert Livingston, made small fortunes providing pirates with guns, powder, and rum.

One of the many small-time pirates who bought goods from Livingston was a Scotsman named William Kidd. Kidd wasn't a particularly successful pirate. In fact, one crew became so tired of his bungling they dumped him on a deserted island and sailed away without him.

No matter. Kidd was a friend of Livingston and Livingston had a scheme that he thought could make them both fabulously rich.

Livingston suggested to a group of English politicians that they could best combat pirates by setting up their own pirate ship. In other words, a powerful, strongly armed ship manned by a tough captain who knew all the tricks of the trade could attack other pirate ships, recover their booty, and put the thieves out of business. This "official" robber would rob the robbers and any profits would go back to the Whigs, the political party then in power.

Good idea, said the Whig leaders, and Captain William Kidd was given command of a vessel called the *Adventurer*. He also received a royal commission by King William of England, allowing him to attack pirates in the Indian Ocean.

Sadly enough, Kidd really wasn't the right man for this job. He arrived in the Indian Ocean to find the pirates simply too tough to tackle. Afraid — or at least ill-equipped — to do battle with other pirates, Kidd sailed around without any real purpose or financial success. Knowing he couldn't very well return home empty-handed, he turned to piracy himself, attacking the unarmed and slow-moving ships of wealthy Indian princes.

Even in this relatively safe and easy trade, Kidd was again the victim of bad luck, bad judgment, and bad timing.

Although most of his intended victims usually escaped through greater sail power or by a modest of force, Kidd did manage to capture a few ships. One particularly rich prize was a vessel financed by members of an Indian state that had just signed a treaty with the powerful East India Company of England.

The English owners of the company were furious, especially when they discovered that Kidd still carried his royal commission and used it to excuse his piracy. The East India Company drew up a list of grievances against Kidd and sent it back to the King of England. To strengthen their case, they exaggerated Kidd's abilities and expanded on his crimes until he sounded like the most horrible man who had ever lived.

Worse yet, the Whig politicians who had supported the hare-brained plan to set Kidd loose on the high seas had been voted out of power. The opposition Tory party was now in office. The Tories saw the Kidd case as a great opportunity to embarrass their political rivals. The hapless Captain Kidd became a pawn in a plot to ruin the Whigs.

Kidd remained at sea while the political pot boiled back home. And he still wasn't doing very well. His galley, *The Adventurer*, sank off Madagascar and he sailed back to America in an old Arabian tub that barely made it across the Atlantic.

When Kidd arrived in New York, his friend Livingston told him of the trouble brewing and advised him to "get lost" somewhere in the South Seas. Instead, Kidd, in his typical bumbling way, sailed to Boston where he was arrested by the Governor of Massachusetts. In the spring of 1700, he was shipped back to England in irons.

The trial of Captain Kidd dragged on for months and became one of the most sensational in the annals of English justice. The Tories painted Kidd as the cruelest, meanest, most ruthless, and most successful criminal imaginable. The Whigs tried to cover up the story and denied they had ever hired him. In effect, the Whigs washed their hands of the whole affair and abandoned the luckless pirate to the mercy of the court.

The court showed little mercy for such a "monster." Captain William Kidd was found guilty of piracy and other high-crimes and was hanged on May 23, 1701. His body was then hung in chains from a bridge over the River Thames to serve as a warning to all other pirates.

A loser all his life, Captain Kidd became a legend in death, for the tall tales told in the courtroom would make him the most famous pirate in history.

A Premature Demise

According to a famous book on English eccentrics, there once was an old man of Taunton, who imagined he was a cat. He spent most of the day squatting in front of the fireplace, meowing and purring. For supper, his wife poured him a plate of cream.

At other times, he believed he was a teapot and stood for hours with one arm bent like a handle and the other stretched out like the spout. Finally, he believed he had died and lay down on his bed, refusing to move or be moved until the coffin arrived.

His poor wife, naturally distressed, sent for the doctor. The doctor arrived shortly and addressed the patient in the normal fashion: "How do you do this morning, sir?"

"How do I do!" replied the old man. "That's a pretty question to ask a dead man!"

"Dead, sir," said the surgeon. "What do you mean?"

"I mean I died last Wednesday," croaked the man. "The coffin will be here presently, and I shall be buried tomorrow."

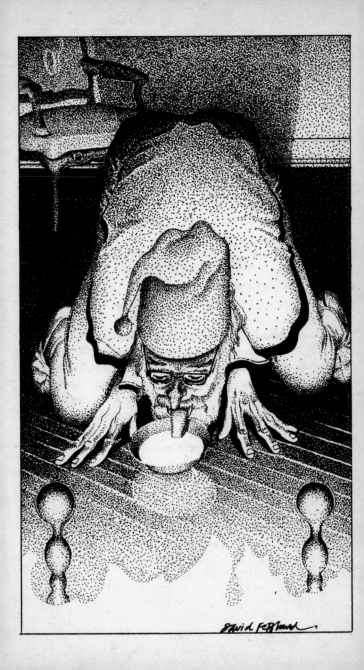

david feffland

The doctor, realizing his patient had a problem that would not be easily solved by logic, reason, or even medicine, decided to play along with the man.

"Indeed, it's true," said the wise doctor, shaking his head sadly. "You are certainly defunct. Your blood has stopped flowing, your flesh is starting to decay, and the sooner you are in the ground, the better."

The coffin soon arrived and the "deceased" was placed in it and carried toward the church by several pallbearers.

The doctor, however, had made some special arrangements along the funeral route.

The coffin had gone only a few yards when a person stopped to ask who was being carried to the grave. When told the identity, the passerby exclaimed, "Wonderful. At last that old rascal is gone — and good riddance too, for a greater villain never lived!"

On hearing these words, the "dead man" sat up in his coffin and screamed, "You lying scoundrel. If I were not dead I'd make you eat those words. But as it is, I've left this world and can't fight back."

A few more yards and the scene was repeated with another man: "That no good so-and-so, he deserved to die," said the second accuser.

This time the attack was too much for the "corpse," and he jumped out of the coffin and tried to throttle his accuser. The doctor, the pallbearers, and a host of village people who had been trailing behind the odd procession all burst into laughter.

The laughter seemed to bring the "dead man" to his senses, for he dusted off his jacket, shook out the wrinkles in his "burying suit," and declared himself alive again.

A Born-Again Aviator

Captain J. H. Hedley, an American aviator in World War I, was one of those rare people who had the opportunity to reflect doubly on the fear of flying: He fell out of his plane in mid-air—and then fell back into it again!

Hedley was riding as navigator in an open-cockpit two-seater plane over the German lines on January 6, 1918. The pilot, a Canadian named Makepeace, had taken them up to 15,000 feet to spy on enemy installations, when suddenly they were attacked by German fighters.

Makepeace quickly went into a steep vertical dive—and Captain Hedley flew out of his seat and into the air!

Unaware that his companion was even missing, Makepeace continued diving to evade the German planes. Just as he leveled off several hundred feet lower, he heard a loud thump and, thinking he had been hit by German fire, looked back to see Hedley clinging to the tail.

Captain Hedley had fallen through space behind the diving plane and landed on the rear wing when it leveled off. As Makepeace did his best to keep the craft on a steady course, Hedley crawled slowly and carefully along the plane's body and back into his seat.

The Master Faker

The distinguished little man with the courtly manners and strange accent seemed almost too embarrassed to speak about money. But the big Texas rancher had no such reservations. He wanted that original Picasso painting and he'd pay anything for it.

"Look, pardner," he boomed, "I'll give you a thousand dollars for that itty-bitty slab of color."

The white-haired man looked pained and slightly sick. "Okay, okay, pard," said the Texan. "I'll make it two thousand dollars, but that's a dang sight more than it's worth."

Sadly, the little man handed over the small painting done in the distinctive style of the great painter, Picasso. A woeful look crossed his face, almost as if he was parting with an old and beloved friend.

"Aw, don't look so glum," said the giant Texan. "I know you love that piece, so let me add another five hundred dollars to the check."

The check had been made out to Elmyr de Hory, a poor Hungarian nobleman now forced to sell off his family's marvelous collection of modern Impressionist paintings by artists such as Picasso, Matisse, Dufy, and Modigliani. It was a very sad story.

Oddly enough, de Hory was anything but sad when he left the Texan's suite in the fashionable Paris hotel. Indeed, as soon as the dapper little man who looked so conservative and proper turned the corner of the street, he tossed his hat in the air, did a little dance step along the curb, and gleefully patted the $2500 check in his jacket pocket.

"Ah, yes," he said to himself. "It is a shame that I had to sell the Picasso. Especially since it's the finest piece of work I have ever painted!"

At the end of World War II, along with thousands of other homeless refugees, a young Hungarian artist named Elmyr de Hory arrived in Paris with little money, no friends, few prospects, and lots of ambition.

Although he had been born into a wealthy Transylvanian family, the war had destroyed the family fortune and de Hory was earning a living as a professional painter. De Hory was a good draftsman and he had a good sense of color, but he had little creative imagination. In short, his paintings had no distinctive style, no spark, and none of the special magic that marks great works of art.

However, de Hory did have one special talent. Even if he had no style of his own, he could copy perfectly the style of other painters. In fact, when he produced a painting in the style of Picasso, the painting looked just like it had been done by Picasso. When a painting was done in the style of Matisse, then it looked exactly like one of Matisse's works of art. If de Hory painted in the style of Dufy, then even Dufy himself might have thought the canvas was his own.

This was an amazing gift—and de Hory decided to

use it, especially since the market for modern art was so good and most art buyers were so stupid. Actually, de Hory started quite small. A few insignificant fake paintings were sold to gullible art dealers and rich collectors, especially Americans who maintained collections in their private homes where few experts had the opportunity to inspect the art carefully.

De Hory looked so distinguished that few buyers ever suspected anything was wrong. He played the perfect role of an impoverished nobleman trying to survive by selling off his art treasures.

Then, in the 1960s, the art market went crazy. Prices shot out of sight. Original paintings by Picasso or Matisse brought hundreds of thousands of dollars. Eager buyers gobbled up anything and everything available.

De Hory responded to the new demand by setting up a little factory to produce "original art." With two assistants, he turned his Paris studio into a modern art assembly line, churning out new "classics" almost daily. De Hory and his two helpers made thousands and thousands of dollars.

Unfortunately, de Hory's biggest deal proved to be his downfall. Some fifty-eight modern paintings worth more than two million dollars were sold by a Paris art dealer to another wealthy Texas oilman who was establishing a collection for his former college. When the Texan returned home, he had an American art expert check out the art. The verdict: eighty percent of the pieces in the collection were fakes, frauds, and phonies!

The oilman sued the art dealer. The art dealer claimed innocence. And when the dealer checked his records, he found most of the faked canvases could be traced back to de Hory. A police investigation uncovered de Hory's painting production line. His studio was closed, his two assistants were arrested, and de Hory fled to the Spanish island of Ibiza.

Once safely in his villa on Ibiza, de Hory decided to tell his story to author Clifford Irving. Irving, who would later be arrested himself for writing a fake biography of Howard Hughes, called de Hory "the greatest art forger of our times."

De Hory disliked the term forger. "I never invent and I never copy," he said. "A forgery or a fake is when you draw or copy something and try to pretend it is real when it isn't. I've never pretended my paintings are real and I've never put someone else's signature on anything."

Technically, de Hory was correct. He never signed Picasso's name or Matisse's name to any of the paintings. And he never really said positively that his paintings had been painted by famous artists. Still, he copied famous styles faithfully with the intent of deceiving viewers. More important, by hints, suggestions, and subtle clues, he implied the paintings were genuine.

Forger or not, there is no doubt de Hory fooled the art world for twenty years and bilked hundreds of gullible buyers. And the French authorities certainly thought he had defrauded buyers. They tried to have de Hory sent back to Paris for trial.

For nearly ten years, de Hory avoided the French courts. Then, in late 1976, the Spanish government finally agreed to send de Hory back to France for trial. Rather than face an almost certain jail sentence, de Hory — art's master faker — committed suicide.

Jerusalem Whalley

Buck "Jerusalem" Whalley, an Irish gentleman of considerable wealth and unbounded nerve, would do any thing on a dare — or for a bet! Gallant, reckless, and good-humored, Whalley never worried about money, life, or limb when it came to performing an incredible feat or doing some daredevil deed. For example, he once jumped from the window of Daly's club house in Dublin onto the roof of a hackney coach passing below. The driver, horse, and passengers were startled silly — and Whalley forever after walked with a limp.

His bad leg didn't stop him from winning his most famous bet — and earning his strange nickname. During a bout of drinking with some cronies at the Hell-Fire Club in London, Whalley claimed he could walk to Jerusalem and back in twelve months. His friends wagered more than one hundred thousand dollars that he couldn't.

Unable to resist such a wager, Whalley left London on foot on September 12, 1788, and walked (except where sea crossings were absolutely necessary) straight for the ancient holy city. He arrived in Jerusalem about four and a half months later and played a game of handball against the Wailing Wall. He returned to London the following June, to the amazement (and considerable expense!) of his friends. The remarkable gambler was now an even richer man — and thereafter known as "Jerusalem" Walley.

Hannah Snell, Soldier

When Hannah Snell's husband deserted her and their daughter in 1744, the plucky woman decided to track down her errant spouse herself. To assist her pursuit, Hannah donned the clothes of her brother-in-law, assumed his name (James Gray), and set off from London to Coventry in search of information.

Hannah found little news about her wandering hubby; but, instead of returning home empty-handed, she joined General Guise's regiment of the British army — enlisting as a man!

Hannah marched north and served with the regiment for several months without anyone suspecting she was a woman. In fact, one fellow soldier even considered her a rival for the attentions of a young lady. In his jealousy, he falsely accused Hannah of neglect of duty, for which she received five hundred lashes.

Angered by this mistreatment, Hannah deserted from the army, fled to Portsmouth, and, again posing as a man, enlisted as a marine in a regiment shipping out for the East Indies. At sea, on board the sloop *Swallow*, Hannah distinguished herself with talents for washing, mending, and cooking. She soon became a great favorite with the crew. Because of her smooth, clean-shaven face and relatively small size, she was considered a boy by the other men.

However, Hannah fought like any man. When the British squadron arrived in India, the marine detachment was sent into combat against the French at Pondicherry. She was among the first in a troop of foot soldiers who forded a chest-deep river under fire. She stood guard on the front lines for seven-day stretches and she helped dig trenches for attacks and sieges. In one of these attacks, her military career was nearly ended for good. She received six wounds in her right leg, five in her left, and — even more painful and dangerous—one in her lower body. Hannah feared that treatment of the last wound could lead to her discovery as a woman. So, with the help of a female servant, she cut open the wound herself, extracted the musket ball with her thumb and finger, and treated the wound with salve.

While Hannah was recovering from her wounds, her regiment moved on to new battles and she was sent home to England to serve as a sailor. She was badly treated at first on board her new ship. At one point she was falsely accused of theft and placed in irons. Again, because of her beardless face, the men began to kid her and call her "Miss Molly Gray." Fearing that they might discover her secret, she joined in their rowdy drunken parties with such gusto that she was re-christened "Hearty Jemmy."

When her ship landed at Lisbon, she met an English sailor on a Dutch ship who had known her long-lost husband in Genoa. Unfortunately, his news was bad. Her husband had killed a prominent man of that city, and, as punishment, he was sewn into a large sack filled with stones and cast into the sea. Hannah's long quest — and strange career — was over.

When her ship docked in England, she revealed her true sex to her shipmates and one of them immediately proposed marriage. Hannah declined the proposal. Instead she went into show business and had a very successful career on the stage playing the roles of men. Indeed, for the rest of her life she dressed only in men's clothes — usually wearing a lace-trimmed, tri-cornered hat and a velvet military coat with great, fluffy ruffles. Later, with the government pension paid to her because of the wounds received at the battle of Pondicherry, she opened a pub called "The Female Warrior, or Widow in Masquerade."

The Princess Caraboo

Fishermen in the little village on the west coast of England were pulling in their nets on a blustery spring morning in 1817, when they where shocked to see a "mermaid" come out of the waves. A beautiful young girl, with dark bright eyes, long black braids, deeply tanned skin, and clothed in only a few strands of seaweed, walked out of the sea and collapsed into their arms.

Revived by strong tea and a hot bath, the girl told a fantastic tale: She was the "Princess Caraboo," daughter of the King of Javasu in the Indian Ocean. She had been captured by Malaysian pirates and carried off from her native island and then sold as a slave to the captain of an English sailing ship.

Although the captain wanted her for a wife (and taught her English), he also treated her very cruelly. Thus, when the ship neared England, she jumped overboard in the night and swam to shore.

The Princess delighted the villagers by performing the songs and dances of her native land and confounded the local government officials and scholars by speaking and writing in strange languages.

News of this extraordinary castaway spread rapidly, of course. Soon the Princess was traveling to other parts of England, and her fame grew with each stop. Eventually, she arrived in London, and, in due course, became the toast of the town.

She took to wearing exotic headdresses of feathers and jewels, and long, multi-colored robes supposedly patterned after the costumes of her far-away Javasu. Wise men of the universities commented on her noble bearing, regal manners, intelligence, wit, and breadth of knowledge. They swore that the strange tongue she sometimes used was a dialect of the Malay Peninsula. In the meantime, the Princess earned a handsome sum by charging a fee for public visits to her apartment on New Bond Street.

It was there, however, that one of her fellow countrymen saw and recognized the long-lost Princess. Unfortunately, the acquaintance was not a Malay warrior from Javasu — he was a farmer from Devonshire!

Indeed, the "Princess Caraboo" was none other than Mary Willcocks, *alias* Eleanor Baker, *alias* Elizabeth Bakerstendht. She was a native not of Javasu, but of Witheridge, England, and her father was not a king, but a cobbler.

Mary "Caraboo" Willcocks was indeed beautiful and intelligent, but she had used her wit and good looks to create a series of imaginary characters that tricked money and sympathy from people in both America and England. Alas, Princess Caraboo would be her last impersonation. Stripped of her title and throne, the ex-royal lady became a humble importer of leeches.

The Man Who Walked to Court

Courtrooms and criminal trials have always attracted strange characters, but perhaps one of the oddest was a man named Corder who haunted the "Old Bailey," London's Municipal Court, during the mid-1800s.

For nearly twenty-five years, Corder attended every session of the court, copying the proceedings in shorthand entirely for his own amusement. Corder was also fond of early rising and long walks. Every day before attending the legal sessions, he awoke at four A.M. and then went for a stroll of eight to ten miles around the city of London. Jaunts of fifteen miles or more before breakfast were nothing. Once, to attend a fair, he walked to Croydon and back on three consecutive days, a round-trip of fifty miles each time.

Corder particularly liked rainy weather and took special pleasure in walking through great downpours, thunderstorms, and hurricanes.

Not only did he rise early, but he went to bed late, and, for twenty years, never slept more than four hours a night. In 1834, on a bet, he remained up for one hundred consecutive days and nights, dozing only a few minutes in an armchair each day.

Most extraordinary, however, was Corder's taste for executions. In a quarter-century span, he witnessed every execution in London and neighboring cities. Moreover, because he had become so well-known to the judges and jailers, he was often allowed to spend the last hours with the condemned criminals. Surprisingly enough, the presence of this strange character with his odd habits seemed to comfort those people who were to die the next day.

The Lonely Sailor

The tiny sloop seemed ready to split at the seams. Its sails were dingy and patched, its decks scarred and pitted. Salt caked along the hull nearly obscured the name, *Spray*.

On the morning of June 27, 1898, when he sailed into harbor at Newport, Rhode Island, in his thirty-seven-foot sloop, Joshua Slocum completed an incredible journey. He had become the first man to sail around the world alone!

Of all the American ship captains working during the great age of sail in the late nineteenth century, Joshua Slocum may have been the greatest. He loved the sea and the tall ships. When steam replaced sail, he still refused to abandon his beloved sailing ships and vowed to continue sailing the seas — even if he had to do it by himself.

Joshua Slocum was born February 20, 1844, on a farm in Nova Scotia, Canada, then a great center for ship building. He was the fifth of eleven children, and at age sixteen he left home and went to sea. Like most sailors of that time, he never learned to swim.

After several years of sailing on American ships he became an United States citizen. His formal learning was scanty, but he loved to read and he had natural talents for mathematics, mechanics, and seamanship. He apparently also had unusual abilities as a leader of men, for he was made "Captain Slocum," in charge of a ship sailing out of San Francisco, when he was only twenty-five.

Two years later, while on a voyage to Australia, Slocum met, wooed, and married Virginia Walker, a pretty, young girl who had been born in America. When Slocum sailed from Melbourne, Virginia was on board as his wife. Unlike many other seafaring families, Joshua and Virginia Slocum never parted again. For the next thirteen years, they sailed around the world, their children were born in foreign ports or on shipboard, and their only home was the captain's cabin. It must have been a successful combination, for Slocum climbed to the top of his profession. At forty he was captain and part owner of the *Northern Light*, a gigantic and beautiful square-rigger that was one of the finest ships plying the Pacific trade routes.

Sadly, Slocum's success was short-lived. Steamships, independent of the fickle winds, were fast replacing the great, tall-masted clipper ships. Regularly scheduled shipping routes replaced the old "tramp-freighting" style of the sailing captains, that is, taking a cargo wherever and whenever offered. Slocum had to abandon his square-rigger and took on a small bark, the *Aquidneck*, with which he worked the small ports of South America, still tramp-freighting.

Then, worse tragedy! While off the coast of Argentina on July 25, 1884, his beloved Virginia, not yet thirty-five years old, took ill and died on board the *Aquidneck*. The death of his wife seemed to shatter Slocum's spirit, and troubles came in a torrent. Three years later, in a small Brazilian harbor, the *Aquidneck* ran aground and was wrecked on a sandbar. Amazingly, Slocum and two of his sons salvaged enough materials and supplies to build a thirty-five-foot boat (Slocum called it a "canoe!") and sail it 5,500 miles north to Washington.

This extraordinary feat brought him some fame — but no money or job. The age of sail was now over for good, and Slocum — the best of the captains — could not find another command. Within less than five years, he had lost his wife, his ship, his money, and even his way of making a living. But it was this very combination of misfortune that would launch him on his greatest voyage.

In 1892, while depressed and angry and unemployed in Boston, an old friend and whaling captain told him if he came to Fairhaven (a small port near New Bedford, Mass.) he could have a ship. The "ship" turned out to be an antique sloop named *Spray*, which was propped up on supports in the middle of a field many yards from the sea.

For the next thirteen months, Slocum worked at restoring the *Spray* timber by timber, plank by plank. When completed, the *Spray* was thirty-seven feet long, fourteen feet wide, and weighed nine tons. And, as Slocum claimed, "She sat on the water like a swan." After a few test runs, Slocum was ready to attempt his ultimate voyage.

Although as a professional sailor he had circled the globe five times, he now — for some unknown reason, perhaps just to prove the superiority of sail over steam — set out to circle the world alone.

On the morning of April 24, 1895, the fifty-one-year-old Slocum set sail from Boston — without power, radio, money, sponsors, life insurance, television promotions, book contracts, or even any great hopes of completing his journey. He headed first for Gloucester, then he leisurely sailed to his native Nova Scotia to visit friends and relatives unseen for years. From there, he turned eastward into the Atlantic.

His first real peril occurred after a stop in the Azores Islands in mid-ocean. A gift of white cheese and plums proved disasterous, for he became violently sick to his stomach just as a storm came up. He barely managed to bring down his sails before collapsing in pain and delirium with his ship riding unguided throughout the night.

At Gibraltar, the British Naval officers warned him not to continue through the Mediterranean and Suez Canal because of pirates in the Red Sea. So Slocum turned around and *sailed back across the Atlantic toward South America*. He sailed down the coast of Argentina, through the rugged Straits of Magellan — facing mountainous waves and howling gales that threatened to rip his sails to shreds — and then into the Pacific.

By the time he reached the East Indies and the half-way point of his odyssey, he was one year out of Boston. It would take him two more years to close the circle. When he sailed into Newport Harbor, he had cruised over 46,000 miles — totally alone!

Slocum's feat gained him some fame, and a book and lecture series on the adventure also earned him enough money to buy a small farm on Martha's Vineyard. But Joshua Slocum was not cut out to be a farmer. He was a sailor, born to the sea!

On November 14, 1909, when he was sixty-five years old, Captain Slocum, again alone at the helm of his trusty *Spray*, sailed from Vineyard Haven for South America and an exploration of the treacherous Orinoco River.

He was never seen again. Captain Slocum — and the ship he had built and sailed alone — disappeared without a trace.

High Wire Act

Early morning arrivals at the World Trade Center in New York City couldn't believe their eyes. High above them, so small he appeared a mere black dot against the bright August sky, a man was walking a tightrope strung between the two towers!

For forty-five minutes in the summer of 1974, Philippe Petit, a twenty-five-year-old French juggler, acrobat, and high-wire artist, thrilled the people of Manhattan with an extraordinary act of daring 1,350 feet above the city.

Petit's death-defying act had been carefully planned and executed. For ten years, from the time he was fifteen, he had performed with circuses in Europe. In 1971, he had shocked Paris by balancing on a wire strung between the twin spires of Notre Dame Cathedral. The next year he had performed a similar feat in Sydney, Australia, crossing a suspension cable running from one end of the giant Harbour Bridge to the other.

The New York trick, however, required six months preparation. Posing as "French architecture students," he and some friends donned hard hats and construction clothes and roamed through the towers checking the

structure, wind currents, and entrances. On the night before his jaunt over Manhattan, one group of friends hid in one tower and another group in the second. Using an old-fashioned crossbow, they fired a line across the gap between buildings and fastened it securely.

Then, as the sun rose higher and the morning rush hour filled lower Manhattan with office workers, Petit stepped out onto his high wire and performed for the stunned commuters.

When he came down, Petit was arrested for disorderly conduct. But his fine was a small price to pay for the publicity and fame he had gained. And, in fact, he almost immediately was hired by a large American circus as a featured performer.

The Dandy Man

The Prince of Wales, a huge bear of a man, walked (or rather, waddled) down the reception line greeting each guest by name and clasping their hands warmly.

However, when the Prince reached the end of the line where there stood an elegantly dressed man, he neither spoke nor extended his hand. Instead, the Prince turned quickly, presented his huge back to the dandy, and walked away.

The man who had been so ignored leaned toward another standing beside him and, in a stage whisper loud enough to be heard throughout the hall, said: "Who is your fat friend?"

The remark — although possibly appropriate — produced gasps of surprise from the gathering. And the Prince turned a deep shade of crimson.

This strange public confrontation between the man who would be the next king of England and the man who was the "king of the dandies" became the major scandal of London society in the early 1800s. The scandal, in turn, marked the beginning of the end of the unusual career of George Bryan (Beau) Brummel.

Beau Brummel was born in 1778 to a very humble

family. However, his father's good luck and hard work produced a sizable income, and young Brummel went off to be educated at Eton and later at Oxford. During these school days, he met the young Prince of Wales and they became very close friends.

Brummel had a pleasant personality, a handsome face, a quick wit, a love of practical jokes, and an independent income. All the traits necessary for the "perfect gentleman" and "man-about-town" in nineteenth-century England.

But Brummel had one other talent that would make him famous forever — he had a perfect sense of fashion and style.

Because he was part of the group that surrounded the Prince, Brummel's taste in clothes soon was influencing all of London society. He always appeared perfectly dressed on every occasion, and soon everyone was copying his clothes, his speech, and his mannerisms — as well as imitating his jokes and witticisms.

Brummel is credited with introducing such fashionable innovations as pencil-thin trousers that buttoned at the cuffs, and the cravat, or fancy neck scarf. (The modern necktie comes from Brummel's invention!)

As his fame grew, Brummel (now nicknamed "Beau" for his beautiful dress and elegant style) became the toast of high society, invited to every important party, seen at all the major events, and always attending the best plays and sporting events. To be invited to the same party as Brummel was considered the height of success in London society. To not receive an invitation or, worse yet, to be snubbed by Beau, was considered a fate worse than death.

Thus, when the Prince of Wales snubbed Beau —

and Beau, in turn, publicly insulted the royal heir, it was a matter of serious importance for London socialites. Naturally, the royal family commanded loyalty and attention. Fearing they might be dropped from the palace invitation lists, most people sided with the Prince against Brummel. (Oddly, no one knows what touched off the spat between these two old friends — but it must have been some deep personal misunderstanding.)

Toppled from his lofty height as master of dandies, Brummel became deeply depressed and, in his despair, turned to gambling. Within a few years, Beau had run through the small inheritance left by his father. With creditors hot on his trail, he fled the country to France. For a short time his fortunes revived, when the British Government appointed him Consul in Caen. Alas, poor Brummel was used to a rather grandiose life-style and he was soon in debt again.

Thrown into prison by the French, Beau lost his health and then his sanity. As he grew increasingly more feeble-minded, he often imagined that he was hosting luxurious dinner parties in his cell, to which great and famous people were invited. The trustees of the asylum liked Beau and tried to humor him. In fact, one sympathetic attendant sometimes played the part of Brummel's one-time patron and friend — the Prince of Wales.

Cycling Circumnavigation

Clanking and clattering, the strange apparition rolled into the little Indian village, scattering chickens and cows before it. The simple farmers stared in disbelief at the sight of a mustachioed blond giant riding a huge wheel.

In 1884, Thomas Stevens, a daredevil American from San Francisco, set off on an incredible journey: he would pedal a bicycle around the world!

The bicycle was then a fairly new — and crude — contraption, consisting of an oversized front wheel and a tiny rear wheel, with the rider sitting high over the front on a hard little saddle. A ride was a bone-rattling, kidney-jarring experience, and a fall from the height of the big wheel could be disasterous.

The dangers and discomforts of this long-distance adventure didn't bother Stevens at all. He covered the three thousand miles from California to Boston in about three and one-half months. Then, just when it seemed a lack of funds would keep him on the American continent, a manufacturer of bicycles agreed to pay for his exploit.

Stevens and his bicycle sailed for Europe in August 1884. Except when absolutely impossible, he pedaled from dockside in France across Europe, through the Middle East, over Persia and India, and on into China. Along the way, he was harrassed by wild animals and village dogs, threatened by bandits, buffeted by high winds, rain, and snow, and burdened down by the gifts and good intentions of people all along the way.

Finally, three years after starting out, he returned to America — with his original high-wheeled bike by now almost completely rebuilt — and pursued a most profitable career, writing and lecturing about his adventures.

Fat Folks

One of the most famous fat men of history was Daniel Lambert of Leicester, England, who was born in 1770 and died at age thirty-nine in 1809.

Lambert weighed over 760 pounds at the time of his death. Although not the largest man on record, Lambert's pleasant personality and good nature won him a great following (much like today's Billy and Benny McCreary who weighed 740 and 660 pounds, respectively, and performed strange feats throughout the world).

Ironically and sadly, it is Lambert's death rather than his life that is best remembered. Poor Daniel died in bed on the first floor (He couldn't climb stairs!) of an inn at Stamford, England. To remove his body for burial, the innkeeper was forced to knock down the wall of the room.

Next, a huge coffin, nearly seven feet long and five feet wide, was built and equipped with two axles and four wheels. This cartlike coffin was pulled by twenty men to the cemetery where a huge grave had been dug with a long, sloping ramp leading into it. By using ropes and pulleys, the coffin with poor Lambert's remains inside was slowly lowered into the grave.

The heaviest man who ever lived had similar problems leaving this world. Robert Earl Hughes was born in 1926, and by the time he was thirty-two weighed 1,069 pounds and had a waist that measured 124 inches.

While traveling with a carnival in 1958, Hughes caught the measles and became seriously ill. Because of his great size, he could not enter any hospital room, so doctors attended to him in his special house trailer that was pulled into the hospital's parking lot. Despite the care he received, Hughes died of complications.

To bury Hughes, a coffin was constructed from a piano packing crate. Together, body and coffin weighed more than a ton and was transported to his family's cemetery plot by a moving van. To lower the coffin into the grave required a huge crane.

Over the Falls

The roar of the cataract was deafening, drowning out even the gasps and screams of the thousands of people lining both the American and Canadian sides of the Niagara River.

Far out over the cascading waters, on a thin wire stretched 1,100 feet from shore to shore, a man with flowing blond hair walked slowly, but surely and confidently, across the line — blindfolded!

Jean Francois Grandet, otherwise known as "Blondin" because of his yellow hair, had a strange love affair with Niagara Falls. An acrobat, tumbler, and famous high-wire artist, Blondin had become famous throughout Europe, but it was the great waterfalls at Niagara that most appealed to his sense of the dramatic, the dangerous, and the daring.

For several years beginning in 1859, Blondin would tightrope-walk over Niagara Falls in every conceivable fashion. And, in doing so, he would thrill thousands of people — and set a standard for every daredevil in the future. Not content with simply walking the rope strung 160 feet above the falls, Blondin had to do it blindfolded, or pushing a wheelbarrow, or riding a bicycle.

Other times, Blondin turned somersaults on the wire or had sharpshooters fire at targets he held over his head. Once, he carried a stove, cooking oil, and eggs out to the middle of the wire and cooked up a passable breakfast.

One of the scarier tricks was a nighttime crossing: he went half-way out on a well-lighted wire, then had the lights turned off, and he completed his walk in pitch-darkness.

One of his most fantastic stunts was to carry a man piggy-back over the falls. Of course, the only man willing to take the risk was Blondin's hapless manager who shook and shivered so much he threatened to knock them both off the high wire.

For his final performance at Niagara Falls, thousands of people showed up on both American and Canadian sides of the gorge. The Prince of Wales, then on a world tour, stopped in Niagara Falls, Ontario, to see the fabulous French madman. Knowing this would be the greatest audience of his career, Blondin dreamed up a superfinale.

To the astonishment of everyone, Blondin walked onto the rope wearing stilts! Awkwardly moving from the American side toward the center of the line, Blondin seemed unsteady on the short wooden poles. Then, exactly half-way to Canada and directly over the jagged jumble of rocks and churning waters below, Blondin faltered, stumbled, and toppled from the wire!

As men screamed and women fainted, Blondin swung out into space — then swung back beneath the wire. He had attached small hooks to the bottoms of his stilts and clamped the stilts to his legs. The hooks clasped onto the wire and allowed him to hang upside down like a bat. After a few swings to thrill the crowd, he climbed back onto the wire and completed his walk to Canada.

The Witch of Wall Street

Hetty Green was fabulously wealthy. Left a modest estate by her father, Hetty managed the investments so shrewdly that she soon built her own fortune to more than one hundred million dollars. So clever and so successful were her stock purchases, that many other brokers called her "The Wizard of Wall Street." But when she died in 1916, less kind people called her "The Witch of Wall Street" — and with good reason!

For all her wealth and power, Hetty Green lived as if she was a pauper. Her home was an unheated, run-down tenement in a poor neighborhood. Her daily diet was cold eggs and raw onions. She wore newspapers for underwear, bought her dresses at second-hand shops, and had only the lower half of her long petticoats washed by the laundry.

Her mean stinginess extended to her family. When her son fell and broke his leg she refused to call a doctor. Instead, she posed as a poverty-stricken widow and took him to a charity hospital. Unfortunately, the injured leg was badly treated and gangrene set in. To save his life, the leg had to be amputated. Hetty had the operation done in her home rather than pay the hospital bills!

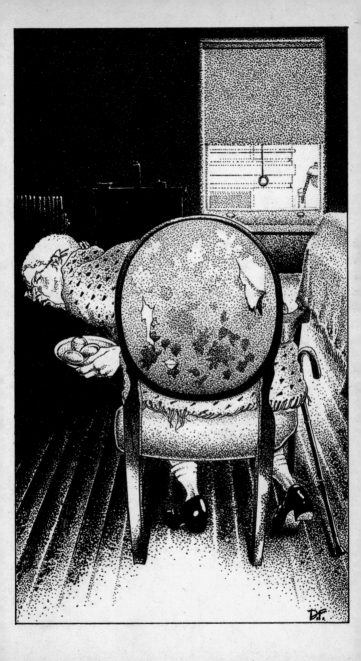

The Great Imposter

The navy medical ship rolled wildly in the violent sea and the doctors and orderlies in the ship's operating room struggled to maintain their balance. On the table lay a young sailor suffering from acute appendicitis. If he wasn't operated on immediately he might die. Bracing his legs for the next roll of the ship, the chief surgeon poised with the scalpel and began the incision....

A tense twenty minutes later, the operation was completed and declared a success. The sailor would be okay. The doctors and attendants congratulated the surgeon. Only one thing was wrong with this happy scene: The surgeon was no surgeon, he was Ferdinand Waldo Demera, the great imposter.

Although Demera's ambitions in life were great, his educational credentials were slim. Under normal circumstances, he would have been prevented from pursuing most of the exciting and interesting careers he desired. However, Demera discovered that his glib tongue, honest face, and winning personality could convince almost anyone of almost anything! Thus, he set out to enjoy a variety of careers, all requiring special training and education — none of which he had.

As an introduction to new jobs, Demera prepared an impressive portfolio of phoney credentials and records: school diplomas, lists of previous employment, and glowing letters of recommendation. (Of course, Demera had written everything himself.)

Using his false identification, Demera became a "professor of applied psychology" and taught at several colleges. In fact, he was respected and well-liked by the students, faculty, and administration at each of his schools. Alas, at one college, a routine check revealed the degrees he claimed to hold did not exist.

Demera dropped out of the academic world and entered the religious life, serving as a monk. When that proved too quiet, he talked his way into a job as guidance counselor at a Texas prison.

In all, Demera held scores of different identities and careers. (No institution ever sued or threatened to jail him, maybe because they would look more foolish than Demera who tricked them.) There was even a movie about his life several years ago that occasionally turns up on TV late shows.

Perhaps Demera's greatest adventure was his service as Surgeon Lieutenant on a Canadian ship during the Korean War. Obviously, he had no training in medicine, but he somehow convinced the Canadian forces that he was a qualified doctor. More amazing, he performed nineteen operations and, according to the military records, all were successful.

The Criminal Criminologist

The two thieves were planning to break into one of the fanciest homes in Paris and they needed a third man — a good man with a knife — in case they ran into any interference.

The man they chose — Pepe — had a reputation for toughness. Certainly, he looked cruel and ruthless, with a patch over one eye, long stringy black hair, and a gruesome scar on his left cheek. Without a doubt, Pepe was a killer!

On the night planned for the robbery, the men met on the street outside the mansion. They slipped through the gates and approached the house. As Pepe stood guard, the first two thieves jimmied open a window. They popped inside and then motioned for Pepe to join them.

But, what was this? Pepe had drawn two flint-lock pistols and was pointing them directly at the two thieves. Suddenly a half-dozen policemen jumped out of the bushes and grabbed the thieves. "Pepe" put down his pistols, ripped off his eye patch, tore off the straggly wig on his head, and peeled away the scar.

"Sorry, mes amis," said the man. "It was not Pepe who you had as an accomplice, but Vidocq!"

Eugene Francois Vidocq of the Paris *Sûreté* was a master of disguise, a genius of impersonation, a brilliant police administrator, and the first professional detective. But he began his fantastic career in law enforcement as a criminal.

Vidocq was born in 1775, the son of a baker in a small French town. He joined the army as a young man and, because of a clerical error, was accused of desertion when he left his troop to visit his dying mother.

Unable to beat imprisonment, Vidocq escaped from his military jail, thereby increasing his crime — and establishing his talents for escapes and disguises. For the next decade, he lived as a criminal, hiding in the Paris underworld, on the run from the police.

In 1809, Vidocq was finally arrested. Because the police recognized his talents — and intelligence — they gave him a choice: He could go to jail or become a police spy. Vidocq chose to stay free and soon discovered he liked police work. He understood the criminal mentality, of course; but more important, he knew literally thousands of crooks and cutthroats, shysters and sneakthieves, burglars and bruisers. He moved in and out of the underworld with ease — either using his own identity or one of his many disguises.

In fact, Vidocq was so successful that he became a full-fledged policeman and head of the investigative branch of the *Sûreté*. In this position, he developed some of the first systematic procedures for solving crimes. For example, he created a filing system on known criminals, and he formed a network of informers and spies throughout the underworld. Even as chief of the most powerful anti-crime unit, Vidocq still went into the street himself to trap criminals with his impersonations of an "accomplice."

In the end, Vidocq may have been too successful. Certain French officials feared his power, especially his control of both the underworld and the police. In 1832, after serving as head of the *Sûreté* for twenty-three years, Vidocq was tossed out — accused of having a crime committed so he could get the glory of solving it.

When Vidocq retired from police work he ran a paper mill and hired ex-criminals as his laborers. But Vidocq, himself an ex-criminal, had already established the basis for all modern police departments.

The Unending House

At eight A.M. every working day for thirty-eight years a full crew of carpenters, plumbers, brickmasons, plasterers, cabinetmakers, and electricians arrived at Sarah Winchester's mansion near San Jose, California.

Their job? To continue building additions to what had already become one of the largest — and oddest — private dwellings in the world.

Poor Sarah was heiress to the Winchester Rifle fortune. But instead of spending her millions on travel, jewels, or high-living, she used it to build a crazy-quilt house of more than 160 rooms covering nearly six acres. Some of the rooms were elegantly furnished with inlaid wood floors, satin-covered walls, and crystal chandeliers. Yet, other rooms were only a few feet wide.

The seven-story building had 2,000 doors and 10,000 windows (many opening on blank walls), sixty miles of halls and secret passages, forty-seven fire places, nine kitchens, three elevators, and three heating systems. The total cost of construction cannot even be estimated, but it probably was more than five million dollars.

Why did Sarah Winchester build such a monstrosity? Apparently she thought she would die as soon as the house was completed, so she kept on adding more and more rooms.

Maybe she had a point: Sarah Winchester lived to be eighty-three years old.

The Hermit of Peking

Two young diplomats nearly fell over backward when they saw the strange figure come through the gates of the British Embassy that hot summer day in 1937.

Tall and thin, with a long white beard and wearing a traditional Chinese gown, he looked like a Manchu prince. Yet the man who approached the special desk said — in perfect English — that he was Sir Edmund Backhouse and he wanted to be protected by the British government in case the Japanese attacked Peking.

The young embassy officers could well be surprised. Sir Edmund was not only a world-famous scholar, but he was also an eccentric who lived like a hermit in this Chinese city and was almost never seen by other Westerners.

Backhouse went outside only at night. And then he rode only in a covered rickshaw while wearing a handkerchief over his face. He was the last person anyone expected to see at the British Embassy.

Indeed, within a few days, Backhouse left the protected area and returned to his "hidden life" in a secluded private home. He would remain there — and die there — even after Japanese troops captured the city.

At his death, the world mourned the passing of this great scholar who had translated scores of ancient manuscripts, co-authored two popular histories, and donated a fabulously valuable collection of Chinese literature to Oxford University.

Also following his death, still another side of this strange man was revealed: He had served as a secret agent for His Majesty's government in China during World War I. Moreover, his extensive personal diaries showed he had masterminded many successful business deals for British and American companies in China. And he had been the close friend of almost every important person in old imperial China — including the Empress Dowager herself, the famous "dragon lady" who launched the Boxer Rebellion designed to drive the "foreign devils" from China in the early 1900s.

Scholar, adventurer, merchant prince, gift-giver, super-spy, hero, and hermit — Backhouse seemed all these things to an admiring public.

But, in fact, Sir Edmund Backhouse, "the Hermit of Peking," was something else. He was one of this century's greatest frauds! He was a master confidence man who fooled everyone — including himself.

Backhouse first came to China in 1899, supposedly to work in the customs service. In reality, he seems to have left Britain under a cloud, bankrupted by wild living. The young man did have a real talent for languages, however, and he soon mastered the difficult Chinese tongue and could provide translation services for various diplomats and journalists. Backhouse also claimed to be close friends with members of the imperial court and a source of palace gossip.

This was a perfect time to be "an insider." China was in turmoil. The Boxer Rebellion erupted in a bloody struggle between the old Empress and the foreigners. Battles raged in the city, buildings burned, and thousands died.

In the chaos surrounding the fall of Imperial China, Backhouse "saved from the flames" thousands of priceless books from the royal library. He donated the entire lot to Oxford, thus forming one of the finest collections in the world and establishing Backhouse as a great Chinese expert. This would also be the last legitimate act of Backhouse's long career.

When the new Chinese government was installed, a group of British businessmen thought the country was ripe for sales of battleships. They turned for help to the most famous Englishman in China — Backhouse.

He loved his new role as shipbroker, especially the high salary, the advances of cash against future sales, and the extra money he received to pay "bribes." But despite the "promises" of Chinese officials — and the impressive sales orders — the Chinese never bought a single ship. It now seems clear Backhouse never even talked with the government; instead he made up the "promises" and wrote the "sales orders" in his own perfect Chinese.

About the same time, Backhouse co-authored a tremendously popular book of the fall of Imperial China. He claimed it was based on the "diaries" of a high court official.

The book was a great success and made him even more famous. But the success wasn't without some bitterness: Some experts claimed the documents had been faked.

The controversy swirling around the book drove

Backhouse into seclusion. But was it really the book that made him disappear? Those British businessmen also wanted Backhouse to explain about the missing battleships.

Backhouse didn't remain hidden for long. When World War I began, British officials asked him to use his "connections" to purchase Chinese guns and ship them back to Britain and France.

Again, Backhouse rose to the challenge — and created a monstrous fraud.

He sent excited reports to London that Chinese warlords were collecting thousands of rifles, pistols, and machine guns from the frontiers. They were arriving at Chinese ports on muleback and in rickety old junks, said Backhouse. Now he needed money to purchase them for the war effort. Money he got, but the Allies received no guns. The weapons were all in his imagination.

The British High Command was embarrassed and angry. However, because of wartime secrecy, no mention was made of their agent's failure. Besides, many British officers believed Backhouse had been tricked by the Chinese, never realizing that he was the true trickster.

Backhouse next used his supposed "success as a secret agent" to convince an American businessman, George Hall, that the American Banknote Company of New York could easily win the contract to print all the paper money in China. Backhouse again received a large advance in cash. And, again, he failed to deliver the contract. (He even convinced Hall to finance a fantastic scheme to steal the royal jewels. But this, too, was a hoax.)

With the Banknote Company hot on his heels, Backhouse again went into hiding. He emerged several years later with a second book based on "court manuscripts."

Again, a few China experts denounced his history as a fake; but Backhouse told such a convincing story about how he discovered the papers that the public believed him — and bought hundreds of copies. His fame as a scholar grew even greater.

As he grew older, Backhouse became almost a legendary figure — a crazy duck dressed in Chinese gowns who lived alone hidden behind high walls in the middle of one of the largest and busiest cities in the world. He was rarely seen, but on his infrequent appearances he was hailed as a genius, a respected and beloved scholar, and a gentleman.

Yet, Sir Edmund Backhouse was a total fraud.

He invented the battleship sales. He created imaginary gun supplies. He duped the Banknote Company. He accepted thousands of dollars for services he never provided. He faked friendships in high places. And, worst of all, he probably forged the famous "court diaries," writing the exciting accounts of murders and love affairs out of his own head.

Most incredible, he even faked his own memoirs. His personal diaries, found in his hideaway house after the Japanese withdrew from China, were filled with tales of imaginary awards, phantom lovers, and pretend adventures.

The Thousand-Mile Canvas

It may have been the biggest canvas in the history of art. Certainly, it was the most incredible journey ever taken by an artist.

In 1840, John Banvard, a twenty-five-year-old painter from New York, began floating down the Mississippi River in a skiff. He carried with him a monstrous pile of drawing pads. For the next four hundred days, he slowly drifted south sketching the scenery on either side.

Back in his studio, Banvard converted the rough sketches into a mammoth painting, on a series of canvases, called "The Panorama of Mississippi." It took five years to complete and depicted more than 1,200 miles of river bank. From the Mississippi's origin in the north central United States to its mouth in New Orleans.

To display the "Panorama" required the use of two large, revolving cylinders; and, a proper viewing usually took more than two hours. Still, thousands of New Yorkers — and, later, people all over the world — happily paid hard cash to see this wonder. Indeed, Banvard made at least two hundred thousand dollars from the display of his master work in both the United States and abroad. Later, the "Panorama" was sold to an eccentric English gentleman and it disappeared.

Row, Row, Row Your Boat

The tiny craft bobbed against the rocky shoreline and then, riding on the waves, scooted between some menacing crags and beached on a tiny half-moon of sand. Two bearded and weather-beaten men, their clothes in tatters, their hands bloody and raw, climbed onto the shore.

No cheering crowds met them. No bands were playing, no fireworks brightened the sky. No reporters were there to record their thoughts. Yet, these two men had just accomplished one of the most incredible feats in maritime history: They had *rowed* across the Atlantic Ocean!

On June 6, 1896, George Harbo and Frank Samuelson left New York harbor in an eighteen-foot row boat, carrying five pairs of oars, sixty gallons of water, and several hundred pounds of canned food. Their goal: the west coast of France some 3,250 miles away.

By rowing eighteen hours a day, the men averaged fifty-four miles per day. On July 15, in mid-ocean, they were picked up by a freighter and their supply of food and water was replenished. They resumed rowing almost immediately, slightly shifting and shortening their course for England.

Thus, on August 1, after fifty-six days at sea, the two men made land at the Isle of Scilly, off the southwest coast of England. Their unbelievable journey had ended.

The Mississippi Bubble

It looked like a carnival. Thousands of people jammed the streets. Musicians and jugglers performed on crude stages. Under brightly colored awnings, merchants sold food, drinks, souvenirs, clothing, chairs to sit on, and cots to nap on. One enterprising hunchback even rented out his back as a writing desk. Hundreds of police and soldiers came to keep order.

Amazingly enough, these tremendous crowds had gathered in hopes of buying shares in John Law's Mississippi Company, a fantastic business venture that turned all of France into a financial madhouse in the early years of the eighteenth century.

John Law, the man who created the Mississippi madness, was a Scotsman born in Edinburgh in 1671. The son of a well-to-do goldsmith, Law grew up tall and handsome, with a true talent for mathematics and an uncontrolled taste for gambling.

When his father died, Law moved to London with a plan for seeking his fortune as a professional gambler. Unfortunately, he quickly lost all the money he brought with him, as well as his family estate in Scotland. Worse yet, he was involved in a love affair that led to a duel in which he shot and killed his rival. Bankrupt and disgraced, Law was jailed for manslaughter. He promptly escaped and fled to Europe. For the next five years, he wandered across the continent learning about trade in stocks and bonds and gradually rebuilding his lost fortune.

Law happened to be in France in 1715 when King Louis XIV died. The Duke of Orleans, a very bad businessman, took over the government and almost immediately brought it to bankruptcy. This was a situation Law knew quite well, so he went to the Duke with a plan. Law proposed to set up a new national bank that would bolster the economy. With the Duke's blessing, he did so, and the finances of the government improved almost at once.

With this success behind him, Law was ready for an even bigger plan. He suggested setting up a company that would have exclusive rights to all trade in the new French colony of Louisiana. The French in 1716 controlled all the land west of the Mississippi, and travelers returning from the New World brought back tales of incredibly rich lands filled with rare jewels and precious metals.

Perhaps Law believed these stories himself; maybe he did not. But it didn't matter, for his sales pitch made it sound as if instant wealth awaited anyone who bought shares in the Mississippi Company. Soon, everyone wanted to buy stock in this get-rich-quick scheme.

More than 300,000 applications were made to purchase the first fifty thousand shares of stock. Law's house in Paris became a giant sales center. Dukes and duchesses, counts and countesses, plus hundreds of commoners, flocked to the temporary stock brokers' offices set up on the lawn and streets outside.

In addition to stockbrokers and speculators, merchants and entertainers arrived on the street. So did hundreds of pickpockets and con men. The crowds became so noisy, so large, and so unruly, Law was forced to buy an entire hotel, turn it into a brokerage house, and forbid stock sales anywhere else.

Day after day the stock sales went on, with the price rising rapidly (indeed, almost each hour) as reports — usually false — came to Paris of "new discoveries" in Mississippi.

For example, one man sent his butler to the market to sell 250 shares at eight thousand dollars each. By the time the butler arrived an hour later, the price was up to ten thousand dollars each. The butler sold the stock, returned the original selling price to his master, and then fled the country with the difference in his pockets.

Hundreds of other carriage drivers and messengers became rich on just the tips received from men and women who had struck it rich. And, naturally, with all that cash floating about the city, robberies and murders rose to new heights.

Unfortunately, most of the profits were only on paper — not in hard, solid coins. The Mississippi Company had not yet discovered the real riches of the wilderness of Louisiana. Worse yet, the Duke of Orleans, seeking to make the country as rich as the trading company, forced Law to issue more paper money — even though there was no gold to back it up.

Some wise businessmen now started to look more carefully at the Mississipi Company. They realized the bubble was almost ready to burst. Knowing that prices could not go much higher, a few men quietly began changing their shares and paper money into gold and silver coins. One man put three hundred thousand dollars in gold coins in an old wagon, covered it with cow manure, and drove over the border into Belgium.

More and more brokers started selling off stock. Panic swept the country. The government issued an order forbidding conversion of paper into coin, but it only made people more afraid. Finally, a "holiday" was declared and all the banks closed in hopes the panic would pass over. Just the opposite occurred. When the banks reopened, fifteen people were crushed to death at the main Paris office when a great crowd tried to rush in at the same time.

With France in turmoil, John Law was forced to hide in the Duke's palace. He couldn't go outside for fear of being killed by angry shareholders. His company collapsed and he fled the country. Ironically, it was later shown that Law had been totally honest. He had taken no great profits himself, and his only investment had been in France. When he left the country, he left everything he owned behind. The great gambler had lost his biggest bet.

The Spy in the Sack

The French Dragoons had bagged themselves a true prize — although they didn't realize it.

In the early 1800s, Sir John Waters was the Duke of Wellington's chief spy in Spain. He spoke both French and Spanish like a native and had confounded Napoleon at every turn by stealing military secrets from under the noses of French troops occupying Spain.

One day, while riding behind the French lines, he was surprised by a squad of French cavalry and taken prisoner. Because he had been wearing his uniform — and spoke only English — the Dragoons thought they had only snagged a regular British officer who had been separated from his company. Two Dragoons were ordered to put Waters on a horse and take him back to headquarters for questioning. The French soldiers had other ideas, however. First they took his watch, money, and gold buttons. Then, they planned to kill him, making it appear as if they shot him trying to escape.

The Dragoons stopped at a flour mill and, so that their story might appear more true, they went inside and left Waters outside in hopes he might try to escape. But Waters had understood their conversation and had another idea himself.

In a flash, he threw his coat over a bush and set his hat on top. Some empty flour sacks lay on the ground nearby, and Waters crawled inside one and then managed to get himself atop a horse loaded with filled sacks.

When the French soldiers came out of the mill they fired their rifles into the dummy officer hiding behind; and, thinking they had killed their prisoner, they rode off with his money and his watch.

A short time later, the miller came out, mounted his horse, and headed for the market with his sacks of flour. About one mile down the road Sir John Waters emerged from the flour sack and tapped the miller on the shoulder.

Waters, of course, was covered with a layer of fine white flour dust. Convinced he had seen a ghost, the miller screamed in fright and jumped from his horse. Sir John, still covered with flour, galloped back to the British lines and delivered his latest information on French troop movements to the Duke of Wellington.

The Patagonian Sampson

The stage lights dimmed. The orchestra struck up an overture and the curtains of the Sadler's Wells Theatre opened to show one of the most amazing feats of strength ever seen in London.

On the center of the stage stood Giovanni Belzoni, otherwise known as "The Patagonian Sampson," a huge giant of a man. Despite his enormous size, weight, and bulging muscles, the man was perfectly proportioned and strikingly handsome, with piercing dark eyes and a great flowing beard.

A dozen assistants hurried on to the stage — and, in a flash, arranged a large metal frame on Belzoni's shoulders. Then, one by one, the assistants climbed onto this same frame. Once all the stagehands were on board, Belzoni — carrying a flag in each hand — strutted about the stage while carrying on his shoulders three-quarters of a ton of human flesh! The crowd went wild with cheers and applause.

Giovanni Belzoni was born in Padua, Italy, in the late eighteenth century. Little is known of his early years, except that even as a young man he was known for his incredible size, his near-superhuman strength, his great charm, and his abilities as a magician.

About the time that Napoleon's armies were marching across Europe, Belzoni was wandering through England as a sideshow strongman. Eventually, he became a star attraction in the largest theater in London.

When the wars ended with Napoleon's defeat at Waterloo, Belzoni — who was as bold as he was strong — went to the British government with a daring scheme. He proposed that he be sent to Egypt and claim for England the colossal stone head of Rameses II.

In 1816, Belzoni the magician became Belzoni the explorer and, with a gang of hundreds of Egyptian laborers, dragged the massive stone head of the Pharaoh from its place at Thebes, loaded it on a barge, and floated it down the Nile River to a ship that would carry it back to London.

So successful was this daring plan that the British government in Cairo allowed Belzoni to carry out other explorations and diggings for the next three years.

He opened the second pyramid at Giza, discovered six royal tombs in the Valley of the Kings, found the lost tomb of Berenice, and uncovered the great temple at Abu Simbel with its gigantic statues of Rameses II carved from the living rock of the mountain wall. Belzoni's discoveries were the most extensive, impressive, and exciting up to this time.

Unfortunately, Belzoni's methods of digging were neither scientific nor subtle; usually he used pure brute force to uncover the hidden treasures. Because he had such strength himself, he used it without concern in reaching his goals. Belzoni thought nothing of battering down walls or destroying an entire temple to reach a statue or mummy inside.

Later archeologists would accuse Belzoni of destroying much valuable historical information in his zeal to find interesting objects. However, in 1820, no one cared about Belzoni's methods. The public was simply thrilled by his discoveries — and eagerly awaited their arrival in England. Belzoni would not disappoint them.

On May 1, 1821, at the Egyptian Hall in Piccadilly Circus, Belzoni opened a display of oddities and art objects never equalled before. Over 2,000 people a day lined up to pay half-a-crown each to see the wonders.

The exhibit was stunning. The prime attraction was an exact replica of two rooms from the tomb of Seti I. One was the "Room of Beauties," lined with representations of the Pharaoh and his gods. The second was filled with statues of bird-headed gods, snakes, demons, and a huge representation of the god, Osiris, sitting on a jewel-bedecked golden throne.

Overnight, all of England became Egypt-crazy! And Belzoni, once a poor wandering magician and a sideshow performer, had become one of the most famous and respected men in England. But "The Patagonian Sampson" was not satisfied with his success. He yearned for more adventures — more excitement.

Thus, less than a year after it opened, Belzoni closed his display and sold all the objects at an auction. He used the money to finance another expedition to Africa. This time he hoped to explore the unknown and mysterious River Niger and reach the city of Timbuktu, then a legendary place seen by few Europeans.

Alas, the Italian giant — the strongman turned explorer — would not realize his goal. In the hot, steamy swamps along the River Niger, he developed dysentery and died before reaching Timbuktu.

An Ordeal of Innocence

The giant stallion pawed at the dirt as the knight in black armor pulled hard on the reins. Both man and mount looked hard, cruel, and eager to begin the battle.

At the far end of the long path, another knight sat nervously on a skittish steed. Even clad in armor, the would-be warrior looked small and weak in comparison with his opponent. Indeed, before he lowered the visor on his steel helmet, the lords and ladies and other onlookers who lined the battleground could see his young and terrified face. He was only a boy!

What strange circumstances had brought these two mismatched knights together on the field of combat?

In the year 878, in the reign of King Louis II of France, there was an old, rich, and gentle nobleman named Ingelgerius, the Count of Gastinois. The Count had no relatives or heirs to his fortune except his young and beautiful wife and a nephew, Gontran, a knight of the realm known for his strength, his ruthlessness, and his extreme cruelty. Gontran hungrily desired the Count's estate.

One night, the Count died in his sleep, finally giving

up to the diseases of old age. The evil Gontran immediately claimed that the young Countess had poisoned her husband. She must be executed, he said, and the castle and estates must be given to him as the sole remaining heir.

The Countess, naturally, proclaimed her innocence. "If you are innocent," said Gontran, "then pick a champion who will defend — and prove — your word against mine in combat."

As was the custom in those days, trials by combat determined justice, with judges declaring that the side of good and rightousness would triumph over wrong. In fact, these trials by combat were most often won by the strongest knight, whether or not he represented the truth.

Now, everyone believed the Countess was innocent; but, no one wanted to fight Gontran, who was a superior warrior. The Countess could find no champion to defend her.

Then, amazingly, her sixteen-year-old godson stepped forward. The teenager had taken the name of Ingelgerius in honor of the dead Count, and he would do battle with Gontran.

Again, everyone tried to stop the brave young man. "It is sure death," they said, "for Gontran has killed every knight who has ever faced him."

Ingelgerius could not be stopped. Thus, on a warm, sunny day, the two knights—one a cruel giant in black armor, the other a mere boy who had never seen combat —faced each other at opposite ends of the field.

Both knights prepared for the headlong charge. Their horses felt the tension. Visors were dropped in place. Lances were held ready. The young Ingelgerius nodded toward his lady, the Countess. Gontran looked straight ahead. Even behind the iron mask, his eyes seem to burn with a desire to see blood.

Suddenly, the flag dropped. Both horses jumped forward. Faster and faster both galloped. The clank of armor and the pounding of hooves was almost deafening. The gap between the two warhorses closed rapidly.

Crash! The horses and men and lances all seem to collide in a confused mass of dust, noise, and flashing metal. Gontran's lance caught Ingelgerius square in his chest. The force of the blow was so great the boy was lifted off his steed. His body flew high in the air and then crashed sickeningly to the ground. He lay still and stunned, an easy prey for Gontran's final deathblow. It seemed a sure end to the brave boy.

But wait! At the same instant Ingelgerius was dismounted, his lance sailed into the air and, as if directed by remote control, shot toward the still onrushing Gontran. The point of the lance slipped just under the bottom edge of Gontran's helmet and pierced his neck. The massive body of Gontran slumped forward in his saddle and then fell clumsily to the ground. He was dead.

The Countess and hundreds of on-lookers rushed on to the field to carry off the dazed, but victorious young knight. For this time at least, the trial by combat had been won by truth.

"The Shores of
Tripoli"

It may have been the strangest armed force ever to fight under the American flag.

There were three hundred Arabs in flowing robes, thirty-eight Greek mercenaries wearing the short skirts of Macedonian fighters, twenty-five artillerymen of various nationalities, and a handful of "officers," each with a shady background and uncertain military experience. For example, there was the English soldier of fortune known only as "Farquhar," and the so-called "Colonel Leitensdorfer" who had once been a Capuchin monk and, before that, a coffee-shop owner. There were also eight U.S. Marines commanded by Lieutenant Presley Neville O'Bannon.

This motley crew of misfits and malcontents had been recruited in Cairo, Egypt, in 1805, by William Eaton, the former American consul in Tunis. His task was even more incredible than his troops: He planned to march 1,000 miles across the North African desert from Cairo to Libya and attack the Arab forces of the Bashaw of Tripoli.

This bizarre — and daring — expedition was sparked by attacks on American sailing ships in the Mediterranean Sea. The Barbary Pirates—Arab brigands operating out of Tunis, Algiers, and Tripoli—had been raiding American ships, stealing their goods, and enslaving the crews. The final act that enraged the Americans was the capture in 1803 of the American warship, *Philadelphia*, by the Bashaw of Tripoli. The Bashaw towed the ship into his harbor, imprisoned the hapless crew in a dirty, flea-infested warehouse, and demanded three million dollars ransom for release of both the men and the ship.

The United States refused to pay. Instead, a young — and then unknown — naval officer named Stephen Decatur and a handful of American sailors stole into the harbor, overpowered the guards, and burned the *Philadelphia*. American warships then began bombarding the city.

Despite the pounding of the walls by naval guns — and several serious losses at sea — the Bashaw of Tripoli refused to release the prisoners. However, he did reduce his ransom demands — eventually going as low as one hundred and fifty thousand dollars.

Finally, after marching five hundred miles, what was left of this odd army reached Derma, a walled coastal city held by several hundred Arabs. Three small U.S. Navy ships lay off shore, and as the ships shot cannonballs into the fortress, Eaton, Lieutenant O'Bannon, the eight marines, and the remainder of the international brigade attacked from land.

Although far outnumbered, the Americans fought hard and valiantly and overcame the Arabs. (But not without cost: Eaton and two marines were wounded and another marine was killed.) The Bashaw of Tripoli decided to make peace with America and reconsider his ransom demands.

Although the victory — and the strange rag-tag army of General William Eaton and Lieutenant Presley Neville O'Bannon — are little known to most people, they are still commemorated today. All U.S. Marine Corps officers carry a dress sword that has a curved Arabian hilt! And the opening lines of the Marine Hymn, *"From the halls of Montezuma, to the shores of Tripoli...,"* recall this far-off battle. But even this was considered too much to pay by the Americans. The situation remained at a standstill: the Bashaw barricaded behind his battered city walls and the small American fleet blockading the harbor.

At this point William Eaton sprang his plot. He proposed to locate the exiled brother of the Bashaw, back him with money and arms, and launch a surprise attack on Tripoli from the rear. He then would depose the current Bashaw and place his more reasonable brother on the throne. There was only one problem: Tripoli was one thousand miles away over dry, hot, uninhabited desert wastes.

Undaunted by this "minor" complication, Eaton (who appointed himself "general") and Marine Lieutenant O'Bannon set off into a howling sand storm with their strange little army, plus one hundred camels, a half-dozen donkeys, and one brass cannon.

The two men bullied and babied their troops, pushing them on over dunes and dry washes. They melted in the sun and nearly froze to death at night. Often they went twenty-four, thirty-six, or even forty-eight hours without water, before struggling near-dead into an oasis and collapsing from heat and exhaustion. At least half the animals died and half the Arab troops deserted, taking camels with them.

Count Boruwlaski

The two men glared at each other across the great hall. The flickering light of the open fire intensified the looks of hate on their faces. Angry words were shouted. Suddenly, one man grasped the red-hot tongs from the fireplace and lunged at the other. His blow missed and the metal struck the hearth with a terrible crash. Further enraged by his misdirected blow, the man chased the other about the room, swinging the tongs wildly in an attempt to tear the very head from his shoulders.

Luckily, at just this moment, other men attracted by the noise burst into the room and prevented a possible slaughter. And they did it by simply picking up the two men and setting one on the fireplace mantle and the other on a bookshelf. Amazingly enough, neither "fighter" was more than two feet tall.

In 1752, the two most famous dwarves in Europe were "Count Joseph Boruwlaski" and "Bebe." And the two men were bitter rivals.

As was then the custom, European royalty often included dwarves, hunchbacks, and other physical oddities in their households. Count Boruwlaski, for example, became the traveling companion of the Countess Humieska in his native Poland, and together they visited all the great courts of Europe. In Germany, France, and elsewhere he was a tremendous favorite because of his handsome features and ready wit.

During one visit to Vienna he was presented to the Empress Maria Theresa. She was so taken by his charm that she gave him a beautiful diamond ring from the finger of her six-year-old daughter, because any ring on her own hand was twice too large for the Count's tiny fingers. (The little daughter, incidentally, was Marie Antoinette, who would later lose her head on the guillotine.)

As the fame of Count Boruwlaski spread through the courts, ill feeling began to grow in the other royal favorite, the dwarf Bebe. Bebe was the companion of Stanislas Leckzinski, the supposed King of Poland. Unlike the Count, Bebe had a very mean and nasty personality and was wracked by jealously. When the Countess Humieska visited the king, the two famous dwarves met face-to-face for the first time, and the long-simmering feud erupted in Bebe's attack on the Count with the fire tongs.

Although the Count nearly lost his life in this strange duel, he really won the hearts of everyone. Bebe's vicious and unjustified attack turned the public toward the Count, and he became the toast of the continent.

The Count continued to be active in the theater and social life of Europe and England throughout his long life (he lived to be ninety-eight!), and he married a lovely actress of normal size. (Whenever she became angry with the Count, she picked him up and placed him on the mantlepiece.)

Perhaps the most amazing feature of his strange life was that Count Boruwlaski — after spending seventy years under thirty inches, suddenly and inexplicably started to grow again. At an age when most men are frail and sickly, the Count was fit and strong and growing like a teenager. In fact, had he lived any longer, he might even have stretched to full size.

The First Clown

What would the circus be without clowns? In every country of the world, the clowns are the heart of circus life. And in circus slang, every clown is called a "Joey."

That nickname comes from Joseph (Joey) Grimaldi, a clown who performed at Sadler's Wells Theatre in London in the early 1800s. He was immensely popular, drawing tremendous crowds and achieving the kind of fame associated today with rock musicians, movie stars, and professional athletes.

But Joey Grimaldi almost didn't survive to become the best-known clown of history. His father and mother both were performers and they worked young Joey into their act when he was only twenty-three months old. He played the part of a monkey in a pantomine of *Robinson Crusoe*.

In one scene, Joey's father was swinging the "monkey" around on a chain. The chain broke, and Joey sailed out into the crowd. Luckily, he landed square in the lap of a fat, old gentleman and thus survived to give his nickname to all clowns in the future.

Ponzi's Game

"**I**f you give me one thousand dollars today," said the little dark man in the straw hat, "I'll pay you back fifteen hundred dollars in forty-five days.

"If you can wait forty-five days more, I'll double your money! There's no risk, and nothing illegal — just good, wise investments. You can't lose!"

Sounds too good to be true, doesn't it? Of course, it is. Nobody can guarantee that you'll get double your money back on an investment in just ninety days.

Yet, incredibly enough, in the first six months of 1920, thousands of people streamed into the offices of the Securities Exchange Company of Boston and forked over some fifteen million dollars to the owner and operator, Charles (Carlo) Ponzi, who promised they'd get rich quick.

Unfortunately, it was only Ponzi who got rich — and even he finally got burned by his own game.

Carlo Ponzi, thirty-seven years old, was an Italian immigrant who landed in Boston with high hopes of making a big bundle. Most of his early schemes — including even some honest attempts — ended in failure, and Carlo ended in jail several times.

Then he had a brilliant idea. He established his official and fancy-sounding Securities Exchange Company at 27 School Street in the heart of Boston's financial district. The office was a sham, however, for he had no "securities" to exchange — merely some worthless certificates printed on good paper.

In fact, Carlo had only his own personality to sell. Although only five-feet four-inches tall and speaking English with a marked accent, Ponzi was a persuasive salesman and an impressive character. He had a handsome, smiling face and a bubbly, open nature that inspired trust, confidence, and optimism. When Carlo claimed he could make you rich — you believed him!

Ponzi's scheme was so simple it was laughable. He found several dozen gullible people willing to invest some money in a "sure-fire stock deal" to be arranged by Ponzi. He then took their money, promising payment within forty-five to ninety days. Then he hunted up several other people and gave them the same sales pitch. When this second group invested, he used their money to pay off the first bunch.

Because the first people were so impressed by their "killing in the market" and by Ponzi's excellent record for "picking winners," they usually reinvested the money — and more — hoping to double their earnings again. Also they told their friends about the great deal — and the friends told others, who told others, and so on. Soon, literally thousands of people were flocking into the offices and laying down millions of dollars for Ponzi's "expert investing."

But Ponzi had problems. So much money was flowing in that he couldn't find ways to invest it fast enough. He was being buried in cash. He desperately tried new — and legal — ways to keep the money and investments alive. But even by making some legitimate business deals he couldn't survive.

Some of the early investors did get their money back and some made a killing; but as more and more people joined the scheme, Ponzi found it more and more difficult to pay back the late joiners. (Actually, if he had taken the money and run, Ponzi might have been rich himself. But he seemed to believe his own sales pitch.)

Finally, in August 1920, his investors started demanding their money back. A Federal audit showed he owed seven million dollars and had only three million dollars in the bank. His game was over — and Ponzi went to jail, again.

His name, however, has been given to all stock swindles of this type. Surprisingly enough, the "Ponzi Game" is still popular today, and it probably always will be as long as people try to get rich quick.

Lord Russell's Punch Bowl

When the Right Honorable Edward Russell, Commander of the Royal Naval Forces in the Mediterranean, gave a party — it was a doozy!

On October 25, 1694, Lord Russell invited six thousand naval officers and other guests to his mansion for a party. In his gardens, he built a giant fountain and filled it with: four barrels of brandy, the juice of 25,000 lemons, twenty gallons of lime juice, 1,300 pounds of sugar, five pounds of grated nutmeg, three hundred toasted biscuits, and fifty gallons of white wine.

Over the fountain he raised a large canopy to keep out the rain and, floating in the sea of drink, was a small boy in a boat who rowed around and filled the cups of the drinkers.

The Tower Builder

In all ages, from Biblical days until today, men have defied gravity and reason trying to reach the skies with tall structures. The Tower of Babel, the Eiffel Tower, and the twin giants of New York's World Trade Center are all examples of this human striving toward heaven. But William Beckford of England developed such a fascination with towers that he turned his home into a monument to man's folly.

As a young man, Beckford had displayed amazing artistic and literary talents. He was well-educated by private tutors and traveled extensively. He studied in Paris, where he met Voltaire, and studied music with Mozart. When only twenty-two years old, he wrote the novel *Vathek*, a work of unusual beauty that is still read today. (Oddly enough, he wrote it in French and then paid a man to translate it into English.) When William Beckford's father died, he was left an inheritance of several millions of dollars, most of it from land holdings in the West Indies.

In 1795, Beckford decided that his family estate at Fonthill needed a complete facelifting.

Beckford liked to work in private, however, so he

first had a wall twelve feet high and seven miles long built around his land. Large double gates were placed at all entrances, and men were stationed at these points to turn away strangers.

Next, he hired a virtual army of carpenters, stone masons, and general laborers. In fact, a complete new village was built just to house his workers and their families. Beckford himself was an architect, designer, foreman, and labor crew chief. His main building plan was of his own imagination. And as soon as he had a new idea or whim, he immediately set his crew to work completing it, working the men in three shifts, night and day, and Sundays too.

The result of this frantic and uncontrolled construction looked something like a domino game. Walls and stairways and rooms and halls went off in all directions at once. Just to survey the progress of construction, Beckford had a high tower raised so he could see everything at once. This first tower was four hundred feet high and made of wood. It almost immediately fell down.

Beckford ordered a second tower to be built, this time using cement over the wood form. No sooner had it gone up, when the second tower also collapsed. Beckford was not discouraged. He told his men to rebuild the tower, this time using brick and stone, and make it part of the house.

Night and day, the men labored through November and December, for Beckford wanted his new tower and its apartments inside to be ready for Christmas. The last bricks were put in place just after midnight on Christmas morning, and Beckford ordered a great feast to be prepared in the kitchen beside the tower. The fire was lit, the splendid meal cooked; but just as the servants carried the trays into the dining room, the kitchen walls collapsed, falling down around the cooks and scullery maids who barely escaped alive. Beckford never even flinched. He—and his frightened guests— finished their meal, even as dust and debris fell on their plates. The next day he set his men to work on building a new kitchen.

As his house grew more extensive—with towers and turrets sprouting from every corner—Beckford himself became withdrawn and reclusive. His habits also became more and more bizarre.

One day he would buy one hundred fine wool blankets and then give them away. Or he would order all the trees in one of his forests cut and distributed as firewood for the poor. But at the same time, after his famous Christmas meal, he seldom again invited anyone to dine at Fonthill; yet, every night, he had a sumptious meal prepared. The table was set for twelve people, with a servant behind every chair. However, only Beckford sat down. He ate one dish and then went to bed.

Just as suddenly as Beckford's love affair with Fonthill had begun—it ended. One day, apparently without any reason, he sold Fonthill with all its towers, turrets, and crazy-built halls, and moved to a new home in Bath.

The saga of Beckford's towers was not over, however. The new owner of Fonthill was an old and very feeble man named Farquhar. After several months at Fonthill, his servants noticed that the main tower was leaning badly and that cracks had appeared in the masonry.

Farquhar was as stubborn as Beckford and refused to leave the house.

One night, at the height of a high wind, the tower

fell, dropping straight down and bursting into a million pieces. A huge dust cloud rose over the house, attracting notice in villages for miles around. Luckily, no one was injured, since old Farquhar and his family had at least moved to the other side of the house. But the concussion of the collapse was so great that one poor butler caught in a narrow hallway was blown down the passage as if he had been shot from a cannon!

What did Beckford—the mad tower builder—think of this final collapse? When informed that his tower had fallen, he merely remarked: "My tower has finally done for Farquhar what it had never done for me."